LEE IACOCCA

Chrysler's Good Fortune

David R. Collins

GEC GARRETT EDUCATIONAL CORPORATION

Cover: Lee Iacocca. (Chrysler Corporation.)

Manufactured in the United States of America

Edited and produced by Synthegraphics Corporation

Library of Congress Cataloging in Publication Data

Collins, David R.
    Lee Iacocca : Chrysler's good fortune / David R. Collins
        p. cm. — (Wizards of business)
    Includes index.
    Summary: A biography of the man who became president of Chrysler
Corporation after thirty-two years with Ford Motor Company.
    ISBN 1-56074-017-5
    1. Iacocca, Lee A.—Juvenile literature.   2. Businessmen—United
States—Biography—Juvenile literature.   3. Automobile industry and
trade—United States—Juvenile literature.   4. Chrysler Corporation—
Juvenile literature.   [1. Iacocca, Lee A.   2. Businessmen.
3. Automobile industry and trade.]   I. Title.
HD9710.U52I234   1992
338.7'6292'092—dc20   91-31989
[B]   CIP
                                                                 AC

Contents

Chronology for **Lee Iacocca**

1924	Born on October 15 in Allentown, Pennsylvania
1942	Graduated from Allentown High School
1945	Received bachelor's degree from Lehigh University
1946	Received master's degree from Princeton University in June; began employment with Ford Motor Company in August
1947-1956	Worked in district sales for Ford, mainly in the Philadelphia area
1956	Promoted to sales manager of the Ford district in Washington, D.C.; married Mary McLeary on September 29
1959	Daughter Katherine (Kathi) born on June 29
1960	Became vice-president and general manager of the Ford Division
1964	Daughter Lia born on July 16
1970	Named president of Ford Motor Company on December 10
1978	Dismissed as president of Ford Motor Company on July 13
1978	Named president of Chrysler Corporation on November 2
1983	Wife Mary died on May 15
1984	Published *Iacocca: An Autobiography*
1986	Married Peggy Johnson on April 17
1987	Divorced Peggy Johnson Iacocca in January
1988	Published *Talking Straight*
1991	Married Darrien Earle on March 30

Chapter 1

A Nightmare Begins

As Lee Iacocca took the telephone receiver from his wife Mary on the night of July 12, 1978, he was unprepared for the news awaiting him. On the other end of the line was Keith Crain, publisher of *Automotive News,* the weekly newspaper of the automobile industry.

"Say it isn't so," Crain said, his voice strained.

Only four words, and yet Lee Iacocca instinctively knew what had happened. He had been fired as president of Ford Motor Company.

"Impossible!" the average American might have said. "Lee Iacocca and Ford Motor Company are a team. Why, they've been together forever!"

Actually, thirty-two years to be exact. Lee had started at the bottom and worked up, from tightening screws on assembly lines to developing, **marketing,** and merchandising each new Ford offering. (Terms in **boldface type** are defined in the Glossary at the back of the book.) He knew every aspect of the business, largely from personal hands-on experience.

"It can't be!" another voice on the street might say. "Why, Ford's rolling in the money, thanks to Iacocca!"

"Rolling in the money"? Yes, one could say so. In the preceding two years, Ford Motor Company had **grossed** almost four billion dollars. That's big bucks in any business.

THE STRUGGLE FOR POWER

But Lee Iacocca knew that there were other factors at work in the massive Ford corporation, as there are in most big businesses. The name of the game is power, and for the past few years there had been a power struggle going on between Iacocca and Henry Ford II, the chief executive officer and grandson of the company's founder. Apparently, based on Keith Crain's call, Henry Ford II had claimed a victory.

Yet, the next morning, as Lee Iacocca drove the twenty-five miles to Dearborn, Michigan, from his home in Bloomfield Hills, he began to wonder. There was no news of his dismissal on the car radio. When he arrived at his office on the twelfth floor of Ford's international headquarters, there was still no indication of anything wrong.

The morning and early afternoon went according to schedule. Lee began to wonder if Keith Crain had been wrong. But at three o'clock, Henry Ford's secretary called to notify him of a meeting – *immediately.*

The trip to the office next door, where Henry Ford II reigned over the family business empire, was a short one. In light of what he sensed was about to happen, one might think Lee Iacocca would have made the journey slowly. But that was not his style. Standing six feet tall and weighing almost two hundred pounds, he always walked with a sure, self-confident stride.

THE EXECUTION

Henry Ford II was seated at a marble conference table in the room. His brother Bill, the company's biggest **stockholder,** was also at the table. Lee was glad to see Bill, who had always been a good friend and strong supporter.

But truthfully, Lee knew that whatever Henry Ford decided at Ford Motor Company was how things would be handled. Not only was Henry chairman of the **board of directors** as well as chief executive officer, he was also a walking, talking autocrat (a ruler with unlimited authority) who had little use for democratic procedures within the company.

Taking his place at the table, Lee focused his attention on Henry. The Ford magnate groped for words. "There comes a time when I have to do things my way . . . " he began. In the moments that followed, he mentioned the need to reorganize the company, and what a nice association he and Lee had enjoyed. Then Ford got to the real purpose of the meeting. Looking directly at Lee, he said, "I think you should leave. It's best for the company."

Lee could hardly believe his ears. "Best for the company . . . " *He,* Lee Iacocca, was best for the company. Had Henry Ford forgotten who had developed and promoted the Ford Mustang, Maverick, and Pinto? What about the Mercury Marquis and Cougar, not to mention the Lincoln Continental.

Ford Motor Company head Henry Ford II ran his corporation with an iron fist, demanding obedience and loyalty from all his top executives. Gradually, Lee Iacocca lost favor with Ford, and subsequently lost his job as well. (Ford Motor Company.)

Creative designs, constant innovations, billions of dollars in **profits** . . . and now Henry Ford was saying that Lee's departure would be "best for the company."

Always, Lee had been a fighter. He was not about to stop now. If he was going to be fired, he wanted to know why.

But Henry Ford could not supply any reasons. "It's personal," he replied to Lee's demand for an explanation. After a few more remarks, the Ford chieftain finally said, "Well, sometimes you just don't like somebody."

There was little more to say. So that Lee could retain his **pension** and additional benefits, it was decided that October 15, 1978, would be the date of his official resignation. It would be his fifty-fourth birthday. Some present!

An Understanding Father

There was one person who would have understood – Nicola Iacocca, Lee's father. Better than that, he would have probably been able to turn the entire situation from a **debit** into a **credit,** a **liability** into an **asset.** Some folks who knew both men remarked that the two Iacoccas possessed a special kind of liquid in their veins – "business blood" – which seemed to be made up of a keen sense of **entrepreneurship,** wise strategy moves, precise timing, and unlimited energy.

"If I have made anything *worthwhile* of myself," Lee Iacocca has said, "particularly as a businessman, I have my father to thank. Nicola Iacocca was a role model for me from the moment I entered this world, and I wish that *every* child might be so blessed with such a father."

Chapter 2

Planting the Seeds

He had arrived in America, a boy of thirteen, at the turn of the century. San Marco, from where he came, afforded few prospects for an ambitious young Italian. Some boys of his age were auctioned off as farm laborers, while others drifted from town to town grabbing whatever work was available. Nicola Iacocca (the correct Italian pronunciation is Ee-a-ko-ka) was eager for a better life.

The boy headed to Garrett, Pennsylvania, his hand clutching a small, battered suitcase. He had a stepbrother there, and Nicola was promised a job working in a coal mine.

The coal mining job lasted only one day. Nicola wanted no part of the air filled with coal dust, the endless hours of chipping away chunks of coal in drab, dark underground holes. "It was the only day in my life I ever worked for anybody else," Nicola would boast later. He had little desire to work for another person, especially some unseen mine owner.

"CALL ME NICK"

From Garrett, Nicola headed to Allentown, Pennsylvania, where he also had relatives. Compared to the rundown region he had just left, Allentown's clean streets and fresh air resembled a place out of a storybook. No more mining jobs; Nicola went to work at his uncle's hot dog restaurant. Customers enjoyed the tall, slender, olive-skinned boy who flashed a friendly grin and always gave a cheerful greeting. As for Nicola, he seemed instinctively equipped with a major asset of good business – a sincere interest in other people.

Before long, Nicola was telling people to "call me Nick." He felt no shame in his Italian heritage, far from it. Around home, he did not mind his relatives calling him "Nicola." But he was in America now, and he wanted people to know how proud he was to be here. To them, he was "Nick."

THE YOUNG ENTREPRENEUR

Quickly, Nick Iacocca picked up other traits useful for any new businessman. He offered to open up his uncle's hot dog restaurant in the morning, work the entire shift while there were customers, and close it too. If there was any sweeping to do, he would also sweep. He was ready to go on errands as needed, hustle customers if asked, and wash the counters and rags. Restaurant patrons shook their heads in disbelief at his enthusiasm and energy.

Carefully, Nick saved his money. Before long, he had enough funds to open his own hot dog restaurant. Again, he applied his time and talents to satisfying his customers. The smile was always present, as was the free-flowing chatter. His movements were quick. "I never walk when I can run," he told people. And when running wasn't fast enough, he was among the first in Allentown to buy an automobile – a Ford Model T.

A Call to Arms

With Nick working from morning until night, business flourished at the hot dog restaurant. But across the sea, World War I had started. It was only a matter of time before America would be forced into the fighting. In March of 1917, President Woodrow Wilson responded to German aggression by calling for a declaration of war against Germany.

Nick Iacocca wasted no time. True, he was not yet an American citizen, but his love and loyalty for the United States caused him to sign up to help.

Not many of the new American soldiers were able to drive an automobile. Nick proved to be a valuable commodity. The United States Ambulance Corps operated a training center at Camp Crane in Allentown. Accustomed to long working hours, Nick did not hesitate to work a double-duty shift – training ambulance drivers and then using his own Model T to drive surgeons and doctors to training maneuvers. Offered the comfort of living at home because he was an Allentown resident, Iacocca refused. Instead, he shared the crude and crowded tents with other servicemen.

At the end of World War I, Nick returned to his hot dog business. Now he worked with new enthusiasm. He had a special goal in mind. He wanted to bring his widowed mother over from San Marco.

Shortly before leaving for Italy in the spring of 1921, Nick opened a new hot dog restaurant in Allentown. He could hardly wait to show his mother.

A Girl Named Antoinette

It was a smiling Nick Iacocca who entered his mother's home in April of 1921. Eagerly, she accepted his invitation to return with him to America.

Nicola had allowed only two weeks for his stay in San Marco. But those plans changed drastically upon visiting the home of a shoemaker friend. The shoemaker's daughter was not like any girl Nicola had ever met. Her dark eyes sparkled as rich, brown hair framed a doll-like face. She matched Nicola's ready laugh with her own warm smile. Conversation revealed a quick wit and a mature mind far beyond her sixteen years. Never intending to do so, Nicola Iacocca quickly fell in love with Antoinette Perotto.

In July of 1921, Nicola and Antoinette were married in San Marco. At the end of the month, they sailed to America, two Mrs. Iacoccas instead of just one. The crossing was not uneventful. Antoinette came down with typhoid fever and had to be isolated from the other passengers. Sadly, Nicola could only see his new wife through a small window on the ship.

Although Nick Iacocca traveled to Italy in 1921 to bring his mother to the United States, he also returned with a wife, Antoinette. He was thirty-one, she was seventeen.

NEW ARRIVALS

If Antoinette Perotto Iacocca expected to become Americanized slowly, she was in for a big surprise. Nick Iacocca did nothing slowly. He was a whirlwind of motion, his mind always clicking. If he wasn't finding a way to streamline the restaurants, he was busy making their new home more comfortable.

"Rest yourself," Antoinette would admonish her husband, "the work will get done."

But Nick seldom heard such admonitions. He was always racing forward, glancing over his shoulder to see that other restaurant owners were not gaining on his lead. Antoinette simply shook her head, then grabbed an apron to help out at the restaurant. "If you can't beat them, join them!" seemed to be her own maxim.

However, in 1923, Antoinette Iacocca hung up her apron in order to become a mother. Nick was thrilled with becoming a father, and tiny Delma soon became a regular fixture in her daddy's arms.

On October 15, 1924, a second set of screaming lungs was heard in the Iacocca home. Lido (Lee) Anthony made his debut. Why "Lido"? Before his marriage, Nick and one of Antoinette's brothers had visited Venice, Italy, enjoying the grand and beautiful Lido Beach. To Nick, the spot was perfect. So was his new son, hence the name Lido.

With two children to support, Nick Iacocca worked even harder. Most of his money went into making the Orpheum Wiener House in Allentown a classy place to eat. But he only **invested** money he had – no bank loans or **mortgages** for Nick Iacocca. "The bankers will own you," he declared. "I want to be my own boss." Slowly, however, his attitude would change.

LIKE FATHER, LIKE SON

By the time he was old enough, Lee was eager to start school. The boy worshipped his father, and although Nick had never gotten past the fourth grade, he preached the value of a good education. "I know how to make money," he would say, "but there are so many things I wish I knew. My children shall know, I am sure of that."

Reading, writing, arithmetic – all came easily to Lee. If his father said learning was good, it had to be good. But there were other lessons Lee learned that were not found in schoolbooks.

"Hey, wop!"

More than once Lee heard the name thrown at him. There were few Italians in Allentown; most of the folks were Pennsylvania Dutch. Anyone who wasn't Pennsylvania Dutch was different, in some way inferior. Children made fun of Delma and Lee at school. Delma took the kidding, being warned that "nice girls do not fight."

But Lee could not always restrain himself. More than once he popped a classmate in the nose for calling him names. But he always sized his opponent up first. "If he's bigger than you are, don't fight back," his father had warned him. "Use your head instead of your fists."

Cause for Alarm

Like most youngsters his age, Lee enjoyed good health throughout his early school years. Dark hair topped a sturdy frame reaching toward the six-foot mark and carrying some one hundred and seventy pounds.

By the time he was ten, Lee was rapidly catching up to his father in height. But in the admiring eyes of his son, Nick Iacocca was ten feet tall.

Then one morning, Lee experienced a strange sensation in his chest. It felt like his heart was ready to pop out. A visit from the doctor revealed he had rheumatic fever. The boy was shocked. He glanced up at his father's somber face.

"Papa, don't people die of rheumatic fever?" the boy asked.

Nick's silence answered the question.

Chapter 3

Dark Days of Depression

Lee Iacocca had no way of knowing just how difficult it was for his father to accept the news of his illness. For Nick Iacocca, the 1930s had been a decade of suffering, just trying to make ends meet. The man had little understanding of how he had gone from being a fairly rich person to a rather poor one.

In the late 1920s, the people of Allentown looked at Nick Iacocca as the classic example of how hard work can pay off. "He had nothing when he came to this country only a few years ago," folks said. "Now look at him."

One who looked saw a forty-year-old man with a loving wife and two small, healthy children. Not only had Nick made money with hot dogs, another business enterprise had paid off handsomely.

While driving around Allentown, Nick became aware

that there were people who might need temporary transportation. Maybe someone was visiting from out of town. Perhaps a car would break down and need fixing. The owner might need a replacement for a short time.

Quickly, Nick turned his idea into a business. U-Drive-It became one of the first rent-a-car agencies in the entire country. The enterprise made money fast, and Nick kept adding rental cars to his operation. Convinced that Ford made the best automobiles, the Iacocca fleet first featured Model T's, then Model A's. Nick enjoyed placing young Lee behind the steering wheel, his short legs barely dangling off the seat.

From the profits rolling in from the hot dog restaurant and rental car business, Nick invested in real estate development. Allentown was growing, and Nick Iacocca planned to grow with it. Yes, the 1920s had been good to the immigrant from Italy.

THE BOTTOM DROPS OUT

Then, it happened. In October of 1929, after several weeks during which **stock** prices slipped downward on the New York Stock Exchange, investors began panic selling. Thirteen million shares were dumped in one day, followed by a brief rally. Then, on October 29, more than sixteen million shares were dumped and billions of dollars were lost. In the aftermath, banks closed across the country, people lost their jobs, and the American economy plummeted. It was the beginning of the Great Depression, which would last until the start of World War II.

The Great Depression changed life in the Iacocca home. No longer did Lee and Delma get new clothes on a regular basis. What they owned they wore until the clothes could no longer be repaired. Antoinette stretched groceries as far as she could. A nickel soupbone went a long way. If she wasn't in the kitchen trying to make a decent meal out of few supplies, she was helping out at the restaurant. She even took a job sewing shirts in a silk mill. "We'll get through this," she often said.

Meanwhile, her husband struggled to hold his family, home, and businesses together. The good years in the 1920s had been almost too good. Nick Iacocca operated his ventures with a basic work philosophy: "Work hard, and when you can't do that, work harder." Caught up in the happy feelings of the times, Nick had borrowed money each time he opened a new enterprise. After all, that was the American way, wasn't it?

But the Depression taught Nick a lesson. "If somebody had taught me what a depression was," he used to say, "I wouldn't have **mortgaged** one business on the next." Nick Iacocca learned the hard way what a depression was – the worst stage of a business cycle.

Lee's Contributions

From his earliest years, Lee heard stories of work and business. Between his father and his uncles, it was daily conversation. Psychologists say that from age one to six, a child learns more than he'll learn the rest of his life. As a young boy, Lee heard the language of business – "income," "expenses," "sales," "profits," and so on. He might not have understood their meanings, but he learned the words, and he could tell that they were important.

Business Cycles

Throughout the history of the United States, periods of economic prosperity have been followed by periods of recession (temporary business and economic slowdowns) and even depression (a longer and more severe period of business inactivity). Before the Great Depression of the 1930s, the government did not try to stabilize such business cycles. However, after this economic catastrophe and during World War II, the government began enacting many regulations in an attempt to keep the economy stable. It has continued to do so to this day.

At age ten, Lee got his first chance to put himself to work. One of the country's first supermarkets opened up in Allentown. Most kids saw it as just a bigger place to buy groceries, if you had the money. But not Lee Iacocca. His enterprising mind was already clicking. With a group of friends, he organized a delivery service. As customers left the market with a bag or two of groceries, Lee and his friends stood at the exit holding their wagons. "Need help getting those home?" a cheerful voice offered. Most folks were grateful for the assistance, and showed their appreciation with whatever coins they could spare. Lee gave his profits to the family under the watchful eye of a doting father.

Entering his teens, Lee landed a weekend job working

at a local fruit market. He arose before dawn, headed to the wholesale market, then delivered goods to Jimmy Kritis' store. All and all, it was a sixteen-hour day, for which Lee received two dollars and all the fruits and vegetables he could carry home. The food was welcomed into the Iacocca kitchen.

Despite his weekend job, Sunday was still "go to Mass day" for Lee and the rest of the family. Prayer played a big part in the Iacocca household. "God listens the same to the rich and the poor," Nick Iacocca would say, "and sometimes I think he listens extra hard to the poor." Such thinking helped the struggling Italian immigrant get through the dark days of the Depression.

Lee worked hard, at his jobs and schoolwork. His grades earned him honor roll status at school; his work habits won him the respect of family and friends. But he had fun, too. He like to play baseball and to ice-skate. He also enjoyed swimming and jazz concerts. And with the rest of the family, he would hover around the radio, listening to thriller mysteries like "Inner Sanctum" and comedy shows like "Edgar Bergen and Charlie McCarthy."

ILLNESS STRIKES

Slowly, penny by penny and inch by inch, Nick Iacocca rebuilt his small business empire. "People *have* to eat," he'd say, "and they have to have a night out once in a while." By keeping reasonable prices and a clean establishment, Nick attracted people to his restaurant. The profits he made went into the purchase of two theaters.

Nick's investments paid off. Soon he was earning enough money to start developing homes in a new area of Allentown. Because Midway Manor was carefully planned, it quickly attracted homebuyers.

Then, without warning, illness struck the Iacocca family. When Lee was diagnosed as having rheumatic fever, interest turned away from business ventures. It was focused instead on getting the high school sophomore well.

For Lee, the methods were not pleasant. Patients with rheumatic fever consumed birch bark pills that were so strong that other pills had to be swallowed every fifteen minutes just to keep from throwing up.

Cotton padding soaked with oil of wintergreen covered Lee's knees, ankles, elbows, and wrists, with crude splints on the outside. Oh, did the treatment burn! Weeks slipped into months with Lee seldom leaving his bed.

Despite the pain of his ailment, Lee tried not to complain. Every day Delma brought his assignments from school, and took his homework back the following morning. He turned to other books too, digesting novels with quick appetite.

It was about the only digesting Lee did. The sickness took away his appetite, and with it, almost forty pounds. Thoughts of playing baseball and swimming vanished, but Lee sharpened his skills at chess and card games.

Gradually, Lee regained his strength. The first day back at Allentown High School was not an easy one, but he was delighted to be back among his friends. His grades won him entry into the National Honor Society, while his character and personality captured him the class presidency when he was a senior.

As Lee accepted his high school diploma, he had already made a major decision about his future. Someday, he planned to be an automobile executive. Only time, and Lee Iacocca himself, could make that dream come true.

Chapter 4

Hitting the Books

Many of the seniors graduating from Allentown High School in 1942 marched directly into the military services. America was at war, and the flames of patriotism burned brightly.

Like so many of his classmates, Lee signed up to fight. He was ready and willing to go, eager to do what he could for his country in the World War II fighting.

But it was not to be. As a result of the bout he had with rheumatic fever, Lee was classified 4F – a medical deferment. "But I feel fine!" he protested. "I want to serve, to do my part." No one listened. A 4F was a 4F – no military service. As he said goodbye to friends headed overseas, a gloomy, disgruntled Lee Iacocca felt like a second-class citizen.

There was nothing else to do but go to college, Lee decided. Convinced that he wanted to be an engineer, he applied for a scholarship at Purdue University. Once again, Lee was rejected.

Another top engineering school, Lehigh University, was only ten miles away, in Bethlehem, Pennsylvania. It was good enough for Lee, but he wanted to spare his parents any expense. "I could live at home and go," he told them.

Nick Iacocca shook his head. Much as he would have enjoyed having his son around, the older man recognized the need for Lee to be on his own. "I'll be home to help out on weekends and holidays," Lee promised.

DETERMINED TO SUCCEED

Freshmen often need time to settle down to their studies. Not Lee Iacocca. From his first day on the Lehigh University campus, the young man from Allentown displayed a rugged determination to get ahead. The bout with rheumatic fever robbed him of strength to take part in athletics. No more childhood dreams of becoming another Joe DiMaggio or Tony Lazzeri, two other Italians who had scored big in major league baseball. For Lee, college was all business, strictly business, and he declared himself a major in mechanical engineering.

When Lee wasn't in a classroom or at the library, he was in his dormitory room studying. The lights stayed on long into the night. But there were many temptations.

"Come on to my room, buddy," one dormmate would say. "I just got a new Glenn Miller record. You do like jazz, don't you, pal?"

Like jazz? Lee loved jazz music, anything from the big bands. For a time, Lee had played tenor sax, a little trumpet too. It wouldn't hurt to put aside his physics book for an hour's relaxation. Then again . . .

"No, thanks," Lee would answer, forcing himself to remain at his desk. What he wanted to do – and what he needed to do – were two different things. The dedicated freshman declined all opportunities for listening to music, playing cards, or just sharing in idle conversation. He was at Lehigh for a reason, and that reason took more and more of a definite shape.

"By the time I'm thirty-five, I'm going to be a vice-president at Ford Motors," he told his friends. Most smiled, letting their buddy enjoy his fantasy. Few gave the goal serious attention. After all, Ford Motor Company was one of the biggest corporate enterprises in the country. It hardly seemed within reach of a nineteen-year-old fellow from Allentown, Pennsylvania.

A Minor Setback

It seemed even farther beyond reach for Lee himself after he received his first set of grades. A "D" in physics? How could that happen? He was going to classes six days a week, even an eight o'clock statistics course on Saturday mornings. He was the last one to bed each night, and he took numerous notes during lectures. A "D" in physics? Something had to change.

For Lee Iacocca, it was his declared major. From mechanical engineering, he switched over to industrial engineering.

The change paid off. Gone were the technical and tedious advanced science courses dealing with hydraulics and thermodynamics. Instead, Lee studied problems of handling labor relations, people-centered subjects.

Gradually, Lee found time to relax a bit. Careful time-budgeting allowed him to study a few hours, then go to a movie with some of his buddies. He also enjoyed going to football games, and even made an occasional jaunt to New York City or Philadelphia.

The Power of the Press

One morning, Lee set out with a new notebook in his hand. As a new reporter on the Lehigh newspaper, *The Brown and White,* he'd been assigned to interview a professor who had come up with a new invention – a car that ran on charcoal.

For the next few hours, Lee sat fascinated as he took down notes. The professor even took Lee for a drive in the car. The eager reporter could not wait to write the story.

Not only did Lee's story run in *The Brown and White,* but the Associated Press picked it up and sent it around the country. It appeared in over one hundred newspapers across the nation.

That experience proved important for Lee Iacocca. Ever since his father had plopped him behind the wheel of one of the U-Drive-It rental cars, Lee had been fascinated with automobiles. He liked the feel of driving, the looks of cars, how they worked inside. The interview gave Lee the opportunity to talk in-depth with another person who shared his keen interest in cars. It was an interview that opened even more doors for Lee Iacocca.

Impressed with Lee's work, the editors of *The Brown and White* appointed him layout editor. In this job, he juggled headlines and stories, deciding where everything went in the paper. At the time, he knew little about the importance of compacting the most content and quality into the least amount of space. The experience as layout editor would be a valuable lesson for the future.

By the time he reached his senior year, Lee was getting all A's in his classes at Lehigh. His goal was to graduate with high academic honors, requiring a 3.5 average. Lee tallied a 3.53. Not only that, he had managed to do it in three years instead of the usual four.

Making a Choice

Company recruiters flooded the campus of Lehigh University when Lee was a senior. Engineers were in demand, and good students could pick wherever they wanted to work. Lee scheduled interviews with twenty different representatives. He definitely wanted to work for Ford, but he knew how the company operated. Ford recruiters would visit fifty different college and university campuses, then hire only one student from each.

The day came for the Ford representative to appear at Lehigh. He arrived driving a Mark I, a deluxe Lincoln Continental that turned the heads of all who saw it. The interviewer had a name to match his fancy car – Leander Hamilton McCormick-Goodheart. Lee liked Mr. McCormick-Goodheart, and he loved that Mark I. It was certainly a step above his own '38 jalopy.

Mr. McCormick-Goodheart liked Lee too, and offered him a position at Ford. The senior was overjoyed! A dream was coming true.

Yet another possibility intruded. The Lehigh placement

director informed Lee that he was eligible for a fellowship at Princeton University. If he got it, his tuition, books, and spending money would be provided.

Lee applied for the fellowship and soon received word that it was his. But what of Ford? What about his job there?

"It will be here for you after you get your master's degree," Mr. McCormick-Goodheart told Lee. "Go for it."

It was too good to be true. For Lee Iacocca, life couldn't be better!

Chapter 5

Into the Ford Realm

Lee sat attentively in the Princeton University classroom, his long, lean frame dominating his chair. Piercing eyes followed the professor's every move as he charted the workings of the Grand Coulee Dam. The man's name was Moody, and he had worked on the project himself. Now, as he explained the entire hydraulics system at the dam, the air hung silent with the rapt attention of the four students present.

Following the presentation, Lee strolled calmly from the classroom building. The daily pace at Princeton was slower than that at Lehigh. Not that the classes were any easier or the courses were any less demanding. Hardly. There was just a laid-back feeling about the place, each student understanding his purpose for being there and willing to pursue his goals at his own rate.

NO TIME TO WASTE

Although he knew he had a job at Ford when he graduated, Lee had little desire to dawdle away his time at Princeton. Most of his coursework was centered around various forms of hydraulics, with a few elective courses in politics and plastics. The realm of plastics was new, attracting many enthusiastic students. But Lee knew the direction he wanted to head, and plastics was not at the end of his path.

Classes were small. Lee enjoyed the personal contact that was possible between students and teachers. It provided more of a working partnership.

The most important part of the master's degree program was completing a thesis project. Lee chose to design and build, by hand, a hydraulic dynamometer (a device for measuring the power of an engine). Another professor offered to assist. "I'll be grateful for any help I can get," Lee answered.

The thesis was due in three semesters. Lee worked feverishly, hoping to complete the project even before it was due. Thankfully, General Motors had donated an engine to the university. Lee hooked up his hydraulic dynamometer to the engine to run tests. Each result was carefully noted. In two semesters, the thesis was finished. After it was written, Lee had the thesis bound in leather!

MAKING A SWITCH

The program for student engineers at Ford Motor Company was designed to acquaint the new workers with every phase of automobile production. Lee entered the program in August of 1946. It was set up to last eighteen months.

The training center was located at Ford's River Rouge plant, the largest manufacturing complex in the world. The place was mind-boggling in size, and Lee quickly decided that the only way to understand how a car was produced was to concentrate on one step at a time.

Few manufacturers of a product own and operate everything necessary to make that product. Most manufacturers rely on other companies to supply various ingredients. Then, after all the ingredients are brought together, the product can be produced.

Starting at the Bottom

Ford Motor Company is an exception to this procedure. Ford even owns the coal and limestone mines that produce some of the basic raw materials needed in the building of its cars. Within Ford's operational scheme, there are departments that handle all stages of an automobile's life, from its initial design to merchandising of the vehicle to customers. At different times, Lee found himself working at an open blast furnace, running machinery in the tool and die department, riding on ore boats, or putting parts together on an assembly line.

Wherever he was, whatever he was doing, Lee sensed tension among the people he stood beside. By asking questions, he received answers. Workers had little use for the trainees, who displayed badges reading "Administration" on them. Many Ford employees thought the young college graduates were simply spies sent to report lazy workers to **management.**

Nine months into the training program, Lee also sensed something else. Engineering did not hold his interest. He liked

Ford all right. In fact, the entire operational complex fascinated him. But working on the design and development of isolated parts bored him. Now sales or marketing – that's where the action was – working with people, not machines. What would the people at Ford think?

Lee's superiors agreed that if he did not want to become an engineer at Ford, continuing the trainee program was foolish. But if he was serious about breaking into sales, he would have to do it on his own. "Good luck!" they wished him.

With a letter of recommendation from the Ford people at Dearborn, Lee headed back east. He lined up interviews with Ford sales managers in the New York City area. "Don't call us. We'll call you," became the pattern. But one district manager outside of Philadelphia took a chance. He hired Lee to work with fleet purchasing agents on the types of new cars they wanted to buy. It was a start.

Building Skills

Lee learned quickly that being a good salesman was not as easy as it looked. Operating from a desk in Chester, Pennsylvania, Lee called up district car dealers every day. Often, they called him. When he wasn't talking on the telephone, he was practicing his sales pitch. He hated to have people turn him down.

For several years after World War II ended, the automobile market was very hot. Service men and women, after being discharged, needed a vehicle to look for a job. Car production had been curtailed during the war, but now brand new cars were rolling off assembly lines at a rapid rate. And used cars were being sought as trade-ins on new models.

Lee was troubled by some of the things he saw in the automobile business. Individual car dealers often jacked up the prices on new models, paying little attention to the manufacturers' list prices. Trade-in prices were hiked up too. Naive customers, eager to buy, were often hoodwinked by devious car dealers. In his own way, Lee tried to convince the dealers to be honest. "Satisfied customers will come back again," he declared.

Making Friends

Lee's quick smile and ever-developing gift of gab won him friends quickly. People liked him, and he obviously liked them back. By 1949, he was a zone manager in Wilkes-Barre, Pennsylvania. His job was to deal effectively with eighteen Ford dealers in the area.

Knowing he had a lot to learn about salesmanship, Lee was always on the lookout for pointers. Murray Kester was the sales manager for a Ford dealership in Wilkes-Barre who provided some worthy tips.

"Wait about thirty days after somebody buys a new car," suggested Kester, "then call him up and ask how his friends like the new car." Lee listened closely. Kester pointed out that if you asked the customer how *he* liked the car, he would probably come up with a complaint. But by asking how his friends liked it, he'd likely be complimentary. Sometimes he might even supply names and telephone numbers of those friends who liked the car most!

Charlie Beacham, a Ford regional manager, was another big help to Lee. Beacham was quick with a story and a handshake. "Be willing to admit it when you've made a mistake," Charlie advised. "Then, see that you don't make it again." The advice made sense to Lee. "And don't do all the talking when you're selling anything to folks," the regional manager said. "Let them talk too, so they have a chance to help you sell them a car. A good product doesn't need to be stuffed down anyone's throat."

Lee liked working with Charlie Beacham. He was a fine teacher, a good role model. As the supervisor for Ford's East Coast territory, Charlie put Lee on the road, traveling around from dealer to dealer. When a new handbook was needed to teach dealers ways of selling trucks, Lee put it together. The handbook, *Hiring and Training Truck Salesmen,* was an instant success.

Time for a Slump

Ford dealers up and down the East Coast liked Lee Iacocca – and he liked them. To sharpen his communications skills even more, he took a special course on "How to Make Friends and Influence People." He also stopped using the name Lido in his business relationships because it took so much time having to spell out both his first and last names. His father understood, and that was important to Lee.

Although Lee's future as a Ford salesman looked very promising, a recession in the early 1950s caused a setback. Many of Lee's friends lost their jobs, and he was demoted. But Lee wasn't about to give up. Instead, he worked even harder. By 1953, he was assistant sales manager of the Philadelphia district. For some reason that no one really understood, it was a tough territory in which to sell Fords. However, an energetic Lee Iacocca was about to make the top officials at Ford notice what a super business whiz they had working for them in Philadelphia.

Chapter 6

A Rung at a Time

Before the year 1956, the Philadelphia district ranked dead last in Ford sales in districts in the United States. Now and then spectacular efforts by the area's sales force would push the numbers up a bit, but they never remained there for long.

Enter Lee Iacocca with a creative new business idea. He labeled it "56 for 56," and it was as simple as it was popular. Car buyers were offered a deal in which they put twenty percent down on a new Ford with monthly payments of fifty-six dollars over a period of three years. "56 for 56." Would it work? No one hoped so more than its creator.

As for Ford itself, it was promoting auto safety in 1956. The company introduced crash padding for the dashboard, hoping to lure customers that way.

"56 for 56" took off like a rocketship. New-car financing was just gaining wide acceptance, and Lee's idea enjoyed perfect timing. In only three months, the Ford sales district in

Philadelphia leaped from last place in the nation to first. It even attracted the attention of company vice-president Robert McNamara, who immediately wanted to know more about "this Lee Iacocca fellow."

The "56 for 56" offer was quickly put into the national campaign to sell new Fords. Before it was finished, it was estimated that Lee's innovation increased Ford sales by 75,000 cars.

A PROMOTION AND A WIFE

In the midst of enjoying the spotlight for his sales idea, Lee received good news. He was promoted to the position of sales manager of the Ford district in Washington, D.C. Life was now smiling on the cheerful young man from Allentown, Pennsylvania.

In a sense, Ford provided Lee with still another bonus in 1956. Several years earlier, he had met a company secretary in Philadelphia when the 1949 Ford models were introduced. Mary McLeary was quick and clever in conversation, poised and polished in appearance, and soon the light in Lee's eye. Whenever he was not traveling, he would call Mary for a night of dinner and dancing, or perhaps a play or a movie. Feeling that his new job in Washington did not require him to travel as much, Lee asked Mary to marry him. She did so on September 29, 1956, at St. Robert's Catholic Church in Chester.

But before he had time to really settle in with his duties in the Ford office in Washington, Lee was summoned back

Mary McLeary was a smiling secretary for the Ford Motor Company when she met Lee in 1949. They were married on September 29, 1956, in Chester, Pennsylvania.

to Dearborn. Even bigger plans awaited the enterprising new-lywed. He was asked to head up the national truck marketing campaign.

CLIMBING THE LADDER

Lee's boss in Dearborn was a familiar face, and a man who Lee enjoyed working under. Charlie Beacham had been promoted to head of car and truck sales. "I thought you might like to come along for the ride!" he quipped. "Right now it will be trucks for you, but who knows what's ahead down the road."

It was soon clear that Charlie Beacham knew exactly what lay ahead for his protegé. After a year of spearheading national truck sales for Ford, Lee moved into car marketing. He proved a natural, especially at being able to motivate gatherings of dealers. "You have to believe in your product," he insisted, "and that will come through to your customers. You just can't fake sincerity, and you can't beat sincerity as an effective tool for selling a product."

Heading for the Top

Early in 1960, Lee was promoted to director of marketing for both car and truck national divisions. He was moving up the corporate ladder. And while he stood on each rung, he turned in the best performance possible. He watched some executives fail because they were so busy looking ahead that they were not fulfilling the tasks at hand. Despite his eventual hopes and dreams for the future, Lee knew he had to prove himself capable at one level before moving on to the next.

Lee did exactly that. Car and truck sales showed a steady increase, nothing overly dramatic, but enough to reflect Lee's abilities. As he had done in 1956, Robert McNamara again took notice of Lee and was impressed by what he saw. On November 10, 1960, McNamara became president of Ford Motor Company. On that same day, Lee Iacocca took over McNamara's job as vice-president and general manager of the Ford Division. During his college years, Lee had expressed the hope of becoming a Ford vice-president by the time he was thirty-five. He'd missed his prediction by one year; Lee was thirty-six.

The next five years were, in Lee Iacocca's words, "the most rewarding of my life. I couldn't wait to get to work in the morning. At night, I didn't want to leave." Not only did Lee see himself as a manager and a salesman, he also saw himself as an "artist." With his colleagues, Lee wanted to create "masterpieces" for the road. Analyzing the marketing research, Lee recognized the potential of tapping the youth market. How? The new Ford had to display great style, strong performance, and a low price. That was what young, potential buyers wanted in a new car.

Each day Lee looked at new designs, adding and subtracting features he sensed the audience would want or reject. Models were tried on the test track. Some ideas worked, others failed. Progress. Moving forward. That was the direction for Lee Iacocca. He wanted a sure success. Ford executives were still shaking their heads in disappointment over the recently released Ford Edsel, a model destined for dismal failure.

"No more Edsels!" was Lee's driving thought. The next Ford model was going to be a winner!

The "Father of the Mustang"

Working under the wraps of silence and secrecy, Lee supervised the development of a new model called the Cougar. It was an alternative to the General Motors' sporty Corvair Monza and a moderately priced version of the Ford Thunderbird. Streamlined without being overly flashy, the car would promise quality driving at a reasonable price.

As Lee carefully supervised the development of the new vehicle, he also decided to highlight its public introduction. Most

No new automobile was ever introduced with as much media blitz as was the Ford Mustang in 1964. For his efforts in its engineering, design, and development, Lee earned the title "Father of the Mustang." (Ford Motor Company.)

new car models were revealed in the fall. To gain a maximum media spotlight, Lee lined up a newspaper and television marketing blitz for March.

On March 9, 1964, the new Mustang (the working name Cougar was cast away as less dramatic) made its debut. "Oooh!" and "Aaah-h!" were the typical reactions from media officials, as well as Ford people who were unaware of the entire project. Thanks to Mustang being the sole automobile release in the spring, the new car captured the front covers of both *Time* and *Newsweek* magazines, two national periodicals whose circulations number in the millions.

But would the spectacular kickoff publicity campaign for the new Mustang translate into sales? That was the real question.

The answer came swiftly. Much to Lee's delight, people across the country traveled to their Ford dealerships and ordered Mustangs. It wasn't just the young buyer, however, but longtime, experienced drivers as well. During the next twelve months, some 419,000 Mustangs were sold, a record number for a first-year model.

Henry Ford II knew he had a winner with the Mustang. And he also knew he had something special in Lee Iacocca, who was considered "the father of the Mustang." In 1965, Lee took over as vice-president for the planning, producing, and marketing of all cars and trucks in the Ford and Lincoln-Mercury divisions.

Reaching the Top

Following his latest promotion, it was a proud and happy Lee Iacocca who marched through the doors of the sprawling Ford World Headquarters Building in Dearborn. "When you make it to the 'Glass House'," folks had told him, "you've made it to the top." Lee enjoyed the feeling, but he knew he would have to produce to stay there. "It's like any major business corporation in that there is always someone ready to take over your job if you appear to falter. Every day demands 100% of effort." Lee was ready to deliver 100% of effort to his job, 110% if necessary.

It didn't take Lee long to come up with new ideas to liven up the Lincoln-Mercury line, which had been lagging behind in sales. Since he hadn't used the name Cougar for the Ford model, he brought it back for the Mercury line. "It was for the Mustang driver who was ready for something a little plusher than the Mustang." To compete with the classy Buick and Oldsmobile models put out by General Motors, Lee introduced the sleek, glamorous Mercury Marquis. In April of 1968, the luxury Lincoln Mark III came out, designed to take away from Cadillac sales.

In 1969, Henry Ford II restructured the top leadership within his company. Lee and two others were asked to share a three-pronged presidency. The plan didn't work, however, so Ford named Lee the sole president of Ford Motor Company on December 10, 1970.

TAKING CHARGE

Lee wasted no time in his new position. He quickly instituted a program designed to streamline production and reduce costs. His top assistants were instructed to simplify products produced by Ford, cut designing costs, avoid timing foul-ups, and throw out old-fashioned ways of doing business. If something was *not* going to bring in profits, it was a loser and shucked.

In his office, Lee was demanding. His door was always open to Ford employees, from those at the top of the corporate ladder all the way down to the newest assembly line worker. Visitors to the Iacocca office in the Glass House found its occupant a blunt speaking, tough executive, willing to emphasize his ideas and feelings with strong language. With a Monte Carlo Havana cigar in his hand, he was the typical company boss.

At home, Lee would toss aside the complex duties of his position. He enjoyed working crossword puzzles, a competitive night of poker with friends, a weekend of duck hunting, or a night surprising Mary with an Italian dish he had prepared.

Lee was a loving father, too. On June 29, 1959, Katherine had joined the Iacocca household, followed by Lia on July 16, 1964. No matter what the pressures at the company were, they were completely forgotten when Lee was with his two daughters.

Having been so successful in designing and developing new cars previously, Lee wanted to maintain his record. As president, he supervised the new Pinto model, as well as the Fiesta, a front-wheel drive automobile priced to attract those who were looking for an economical car. Both new models became quick money-makers, but the Pinto proved to have gas-tank leakage problems. Over a million of the vehicles had to be recalled.

THE FALL FROM GRACE

Problems with the Pinto were only one of Lee's difficulties as Ford president. **Competition** from foreign **imports** increased, gas prices rose, and the federal government mandated safety and antipollution standards.

Feverishly, Lee dealt with each problem as it arose. His workaholic tendencies proved vital. Few executives seemed able to survive with less sleep or to keep so many different facts and figures clear in one's head.

Lee and Mary share a few poolside moments with their two daughters, Kathi and Lia, during the summer of 1973.

But there was one problem that Lee could not solve. Not only did Lee enjoy the respect of those with whom he worked, he had also become a celebrity to millions of people. His personal promotion of new Ford products in advertising campaigns made him a familiar face across the nation. Just about everyone recognized the value of Lee's flamboyant showmanship in selling Ford products. But there was one occupant in the Glass House who had lost his liking for Lee. That person was Henry Ford II.

It is impossible to know when Ford first decided that Lee Iacocca had to go. Sometime in the mid-1970s, Lee began to hear that investigators were asking questions, looking into every phase of his business actions. More directly, Lee found his decisions being challenged, his ideas questioned at every turn. Who was doing it – and why? So often the answers led back to Henry Ford II.

Then came that fateful July night in 1978 when Lee received a phone call at home. Without warning, his world came crashing down.

Chapter 7

Starting Over

Lee Iacocca eased his car into the warehouse parking spot. It was a structure several miles from the grand and glamorous Glass House that Lee had come to call his business home. As agreed, he would stay on at Ford from July until October 15, 1978, his official resignation date and his fifty-fourth birthday. He knew the months would be painful, yet he was not about to sacrifice the accumulated benefits an earlier departure would mean.

ANGER EVERYWHERE

The dismissal of Lee Iacocca from Ford was big news. Major television networks picked it up, and the firing made the front pages of newspapers across the country and beyond. An editorial in the *Automotive News* mentioned Lee's million-dollar annual salary at Ford, noting that "by all standards he earned every penny." Other columnists and editors harpooned Henry Ford II, questioning his motives and business sense. One labeled Ford a "60-year-old adolescent" and posed the question, "If a guy like Iacocca's job isn't safe, is yours?"

The media wasn't the only group upset about Lee's firing, for he had become a special friend to them. His constant willingness to share news, as well as his personal association with his products set him apart from other distant and cold corporate executives. That's what outraged Ford dealers across the country, too. Even as president of Ford, Lee was one of them. Angry callers bombarded the Glass House, while letters of complaint arrived by the bushel.

All this display of support and affection was comforting to Lee Iacocca, yet it still did not give him a job. And that's what he really wanted. That's what he needed. At fifty-four, the former company president was not about to quit working — not if he could help it.

FINDING A NEW NICHE

When a business leader of Lee Iacocca's stature becomes available for hiring, he is usually swamped with job offers. Lee was no exception. But he didn't want to jump into a position he wouldn't like. "You have got to enjoy what you're doing to put your best effort into it," he said often. "Getting a big salary doesn't mean a thing if you're miserable doing what you're doing."

Scanning over the many job descriptions and offers he

received, Lee weighed the many possibilities. Several business schools wanted him to become their dean, including the prestigious New York University. Lockheed International was interested, too. But Lee knew where he wanted to be – in the world of cars. Despite the troubles Chrysler Corporation had been having, an offer from that company appeared to be the most appealing. Lee Iacocca was a man who liked a challenge.

IN CHARGE – AGAIN

On November 2, 1978, Lee officially became president and chief executive officer at Chrysler Corporation. Although he forfeited his **severance pay** from Ford by joining a competitor, Chrysler agreed to pay him the 1.5 million dollars he had lost.

When Lee jumped into the driver's seat at Chrysler, the company had just suffered a $158-million-dollar quarterly loss. **Bankruptcy** was possible. It was clear that major changes were needed. Lee wasted no time.

Sizing up the Problems

Lee Iacocca gazed down at the piece of paper on his desk. A shrewd evaluator, he had quickly analyzed the areas of weakness at Chrysler Corporation. The list was frightening: too many top executives, low morale at all levels, deteriorating equipment and plants, no financial controls on cash, **overproduction/expanded inventory,** and recalls of Plymouth Volares and Dodge Aspens.

Obviously, some positions would have to go – or, at least, be consolidated. One thing was certain – if any employee, executive or laborer, was to be laid off or dismissed, it would happen as gently as possible. The manner of his own firing stuck with Lee, and he knew he would harbor the memory of it for the rest of his life.

But cash was needed right away. Lee introduced plans to help fill the company's treasury. He arranged to sell off Chrysler's military tank operations to General Dynamics. Dealership properties in many foreign countries were also sold, limiting dealer activities to the United States, Canada, and Mexico. Efforts were made to position better-placed **franchises.** To save on inventory space, Lee copied the "just-in-time" system used in Japan. Machine parts were scheduled to arrive on the assembly line just before they were needed so they would not have to be stored.

The changes helped reduce Chrysler's debt, but even bolder moves were needed to save the company. The right man was in charge. Lee turned to the federal government for emergency assistance. He asked for a loan.

"It's a ridiculous idea!" one senator declared. "Chrysler is a private enterprise, and the government is a public agency. I thought Iacocca believed in **capitalism.**"

"Chrysler has to do more on its own," another official stated. "We can't be loaning out money until we're sure they are doing all they can."

Lee was willing, offering to cut all costs possible if the government would loan Chrysler the funds the company needed. The proposal was debated in Congress, tempers flaring on each side of the issue. When the votes came in, Lee

Franchises/Franchisees

Major companies and industries like Chrysler Corporation and Ford Motor Company have employees located all over the United States and in other countries, too. Some of these employees have individual tasks to do, like the workers on the assembly lines in the production plants. Other employees serve as representatives in their own communities.

An individual Chrysler or Ford dealer in your community is a franchisee. The company has a franchise or contract with that person which allows him/her to sell the goods or services of that company in a particular part of the country. Usually, the company also has district and regional managers who assist the franchisees with their business.

Capitalism

In a country considered to operate under "capitalism," business and industry are owned and controlled by individual citizens. Although the government may provide some regulation, its intervention is limited. The United States, Japan, and South Korea are three countries that operate under "capitalism." Countries whose governments own and control business and industry are considered to operate under "socialism."

had won. President Jimmy Carter signed the Loan Guarantee Act of 1979, creating a board to issue up to 1.5 billion dollars in loan guarantees repayable in 1990. In exchange, Chrysler agreed to continue to cut costs, sell more stock, win concessions from labor and suppliers, and institute a stock ownership plan for employees.

Lee hated to lay off workers, but he had no choice. Thousands of Chrysler employees were dismissed. A third of the company's plants were closed or consolidated. In order to win support of labor unions, he set an example by declaring he would accept a yearly salary of one dollar and slice executive salaries by ten percent. Then he asked union workers to reduce their own salaries by two dollars an hour. President Douglas Fraser of the United Auto Workers was invited to sit on the Chrysler board of directors.

Building Up Sales

It was essential that Chrysler increase its sales. But how? Lee wondered. An advertising agency, Kenyon & Eckhardt, had the answer. "You're the best spokesman Chrysler could have. You have an honest face, know how to speak, and carry a respectful reputation. Everybody thinks Chrysler is going bankrupt. You're the most believable guy to tell folks they're not."

Accepting a New Role

Lee Iacocca had always been a salesman. But it had always been in face-to-face situations or before big groups. Now the new plans called for making television commercials and magazine ads. Was he ready to become recognized across the nation?

"If you can find a better car – buy it!" Lee's public image of honesty and trust made him a natural salesman for Chrysler Corporation. (Chrysler Corporation.)

"Sure, I'll do it," he agreed.

Each presentation was written and designed with Lee in mind – a straightforward, direct approach. "If you can find a better car – buy it!" he told television viewers. In another ad, Lee told those watching, "You can go with Chrysler, or you can go with someone else – and take your chances."

In 1982, Chrysler Corporation recorded ten billion dollars in sales. There was a profit of 170 million dollars. Lee was ecstatic.

Certainly, Lee knew that there were other reasons for Chrysler's growing success beyond his personal appearances in ads. Sales were increasing for the K-cars, the Dodge Aries, and the Plymouth Reliant. Each offered customers a comfortable six-passenger vehicle with maximum fuel efficiency. The trim Chrysler models captured a healthy chunk of compact car sales and received awards from *Motor Trends* magazine.

SADNESS AT HOME

While increased sales and profits encouraged Lee and the job he was doing at Chrysler, he became more and more concerned about his wife Mary. She had always been there to boost his spirit. Plagued by diabetes, she seldom complained. She simply took her insulin injections each day, watched her diet, and struggled to go on.

But the years had taken their toll, especially the ordeal of the Ford firing. When Lee had to be away for business trips, he called home two or three times a day. He always made sure there was someone with her. Both Kathi and Lia learned how to care for their mother, especially what to do in case of an emergency.

The spring of 1983 seemed particularly hard on Mary Iacocca. Her strength slipped away, and on May 15, she died. She was fifty-seven years old.

A smiling Lee Iacocca celebrates the repayment of the federally guaranteed notes Chrysler Corporation borrowed from investors in 1980. Originally scheduled to be paid in 1990, the debt was erased in August of 1983, seven years early. Lee helped engineer a dramatic three-year recovery of Chrysler sales. (Chrysler Corporation.)

BACK TO BUSINESS

Lee took Mary's death hard. Despite his business accomplishments, his family had always come first. Now his wife was gone. He pledged to be the best father he could be to his two daughters. Then, he went back to work.

On July 13, 1983, Lee stood in front of the National Press Club in Washington, D.C. There was much pride in his voice as he announced that Chrysler would be paying back the government loan a full seven years before it was due. Later, he turned over a check for $813,487,500 to government officials. The federal treasury picked up 800 million dollars in **interest** on the deal.

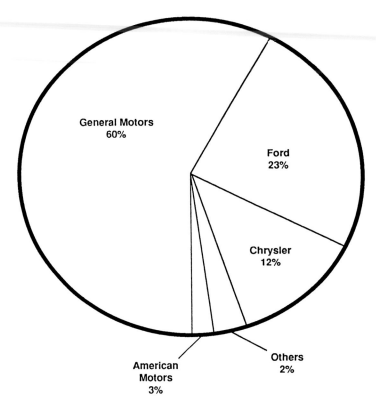

General Motors
60%

Ford
23%

Chrysler
12%

Others
2%

American
Motors
3%

This graph shows the percentage of passenger cars produced in the United States in 1983, the year that Chrysler repaid its federally guaranteed notes.

The Growth Continues

What would be next for Chrysler? Lee Iacocca never looked back, except to avoid any mistakes he had made in the past. In 1984 the company introduced the minivan, a vehicle larger than a station wagon but smaller than a regular van. It could fit in most conventional garages, and it could hold seven passengers. The minivan was an instant success, quickly climbing to the top of the sales charts.

The following year, Lee reached out to Japan, forming a partnership between Chrysler and Mitsubishi Motors to build a 500-million-dollar assembly plant in the United States. The product? A two-door sports car. Always Lee hoped to break the dominant hold of General Motors in the automobile industry, and only a "Global Motors" concept seemed able to do that.

Also in 1985, Lee restructured Chrysler Corporation. He broke it into four divisions – Chrysler Motors, Chrysler Financial Corporation, Gulfstream Aerospace Corporation, and Chrysler Technologies. Two years later, Gulfstream Aerospace Corporation became a part of Chrysler Technologies Corporation. "We are always ready to change," explained Lee, "if change makes us better."

More recently, the top corporate offices have been changed, too. Lee retains the position of chief executive officer, with a six-member executive committee. Often he also pulls in his managers, listening to what they have to say before making any decisions. He terms the exchange "management by consensus."

Displaying and Sharing Talents

Through his television, magazine, and newspaper commercials, Lee Iacocca has become a face known across the country and beyond. His life story, *Iacocca: An Autobiography*, which was published in 1984, put him into the ranks of best-selling authors. All royalties from the book have gone into diabetes research and scholarships, with the Joslin Diabetes Center in Boston being a particular beneficiary. A second book, *Talking Straight,* also leaped onto the best-seller list after its release in 1988. It's clear that Americans want to know what Lee Iacocca has to say.

President Ronald Reagan tapped Lee to head a campaign to re-store the Statue of Liberty in 1983. Millions of dollars rolled in, with Iacocca often referred to as "Mr. Liberty."

Recognizing Lee's leadership and his immense popularity with the American people, former President Ronald Reagan tapped him for a special job during his term of office. Lee headed a drive to raise money for restoring the Statue of Liberty. Busy as he was with his duties at Chrysler Corporation, Lee accepted. Through his efforts, millions of dollars flowed in, and the "grand lady of freedom" was restored.

On April 17, 1986, Lee Iacocca married Peggy John-son, a thirty-four-year-old advertising executive. Eight months later the couple was divorced. Darrien Earle, age forty-two and the owner of a Mexican restaurant in Los Angeles, became Lee's third wife on March 30, 1991.

TRAVELING THE ROAD AHEAD

"I welcome the future," Lee Iacocca says. "You never know what exciting opportunities lie just around the corner." In his role as head of Chrysler Corporation, he continues to emphasize the need for attractive, creative design for products, and at reasonable prices that customers can afford. "Whether a businessman is providing products or services, he is nothing without the satisfaction of the customer."

Lee never hesitates to speak out on what he believes. Looking ahead, he advocates an "industrial policy" for the federal government that would encourage efficient and profitable industries at the exclusion of those that cannot succeed. In the case of industries deemed worthy, federal aid should be extended, just as it was to Chrysler. Also, Lee supports import quotas and **tariffs** in order to protect manufacturing jobs in the United States. An optimistic Lee Iacocca insists that "this country can once again be that bright and shining symbol of power and freedom – challenged by none and envied by all."

Glossary

asset Anything of value owned by a business or individual.

bankruptcy Legal declaration of an inability to pay debts.

board of directors A group of individuals, elected by shareholders, who set the policies and goals of a corporation.

capitalism An economic system in which the means of production and distribution are privately owned.

competition Economic rivalry that exists among businesses selling similar products.

credit A promise to pay for goods or services, or to repay money borrowed, at some specified future time.

debit An indebtedness; money that is owed.

entrepreneurship The ability to organize, manage, and assume the risks of a business.

expanded inventory More goods on hand than needed.

franchise License to market a particular product or service in a specific area.

gross Total amount of money earned without deductions.

imports Goods brought in from other countries.

interest Money paid for the use of borrowed funds.

invest To put money into something of value with the expectation of future profits.

liability Any claim on or debt of a business or an individual.

management Those who direct an enterprise to produce goods or services.

marketing The selling of economic goods or services.

mortgage A real estate loan that generally covers an extended number of years.

overproduction Too many goods manufactured.

pension A guaranteed retirement income.

profits The money remaining after payment of all expenses.

58

severance pay   Extra pay given to an employee on leaving a place of employment at the company's request.

stock   Certificate of ownership in a corporation.

stockholder   One who holds shares of ownership (stock) in a corporation.

tariff   A tax on imports.

Index